# Autumn Passage by Elizabeth

On suffering, which is real.
On the mouth that never closes,
the air that dries the mouth.

On the miraculous dying body,
its greens and purples.
On the beauty of hair itself.

On the dazzling toddler:
"like eggplant," he says,
when you say "vegetable,"

"Arrondissement" + "flower."
On his grandmother's suffering, larger
than vanished skyscrapers,

September zucchini,
other things too big. For her glory
that goes along with it,

glory of grown children's vigil,
communal fealty
of the body that operates

even as it pulls apart, the body
but nonetheless together can make peace

florid and bright and magnificent
as it does, as it shrinks,
as it turns + something else.

# AUTUMN PASSAGE

## 2005

When I'm in the midst of writing poems, really deep in it, that's when I lose track of time. I'm a mother of two sons so I don't have that option much, but I would say there is that moment when I say "oh my gosh, look how much time has passed" and that is when I'm writing a poem. I have time to do that when I'm home at night and they're asleep.

The content is developed instinctually. I labor over the actual composition, going word-by-word and line-by-line, draft upon draft. If I ever get nervous before getting up to read, even at events like President Obama's inauguration, I look at the poem and say, "You're done. All I have to do is let you out."

*On suffering, which is real.*
*On the mouth that never closes,*
*the air that dries the mouth.*

*On the miraculous dying body,*
*its greens and purples.*
*On the beauty of hair itself.*

*On the dazzling toddler:*
*"Like eggplant," he says,*
*when you say "Vegetable,"*

*"Chrysanthemum" to "Flower."*
*On his grandmother's suffering, larger*
*than vanished skyscrapers,*

*September zucchini,*
*other things too big. For her glory*
*that goes along with it,*

*glory of grown children's vigil,*
*communal fealty, glory*
*of the body that operates*

*even as it falls apart, the body*
*that can no longer even make fever*
*but nonetheless burns*

*florid and bright and magnificent*
*as it dims, as it shrinks,*
*as it turns to something else*

# FOREWORD

BROODWORK is the name of the ongoing collaboration founded by Iris Anna Regn and Rebecca Niederlander that investigates the interweaving of creative practice and family life. This cross-disciplinary art and design project names the previously unspoken community of practitioners whose work realized an unexpected perspectival shift after becoming parents.

All creative practitioners find themselves at crossroads throughout their life; however, being affected by the specific juncture of practice and family is not generally acknowledged for its true impact. Who would have thought that writing for his son about a bear named Winnie-the-Pooh would catapult the political satirist A. A. Milne from *Punch* magazine into the stratosphere of literary history. His era's exception is our rule; more and more, the convergence of family and practice is embraced by this community as an indispensable influence to produce profound and unexpected work.

Exploring this work within the parameters of an exhibition is one of BROODWORK'S prime expressions. For each curatorial installation, Regn and Niederlander work hand-in-hand with creative practitioners—artists, architects, designers, writers, and filmmakers—to facilitate an entirely new conception of specific works within their practice.

The installations also incorporate participatory works that are chosen to foreground the intergenerational and community-building aspects of BROODWORK. Through its multi-faceted approach of talking, blogging, designing, event-making, and curating, the project exists not only to investigate and illuminate, but to foster an advantageous environment that will in itself stimulate innovation.

# JUNCTURE

JING LIU AND FLORIAN IDENBURG

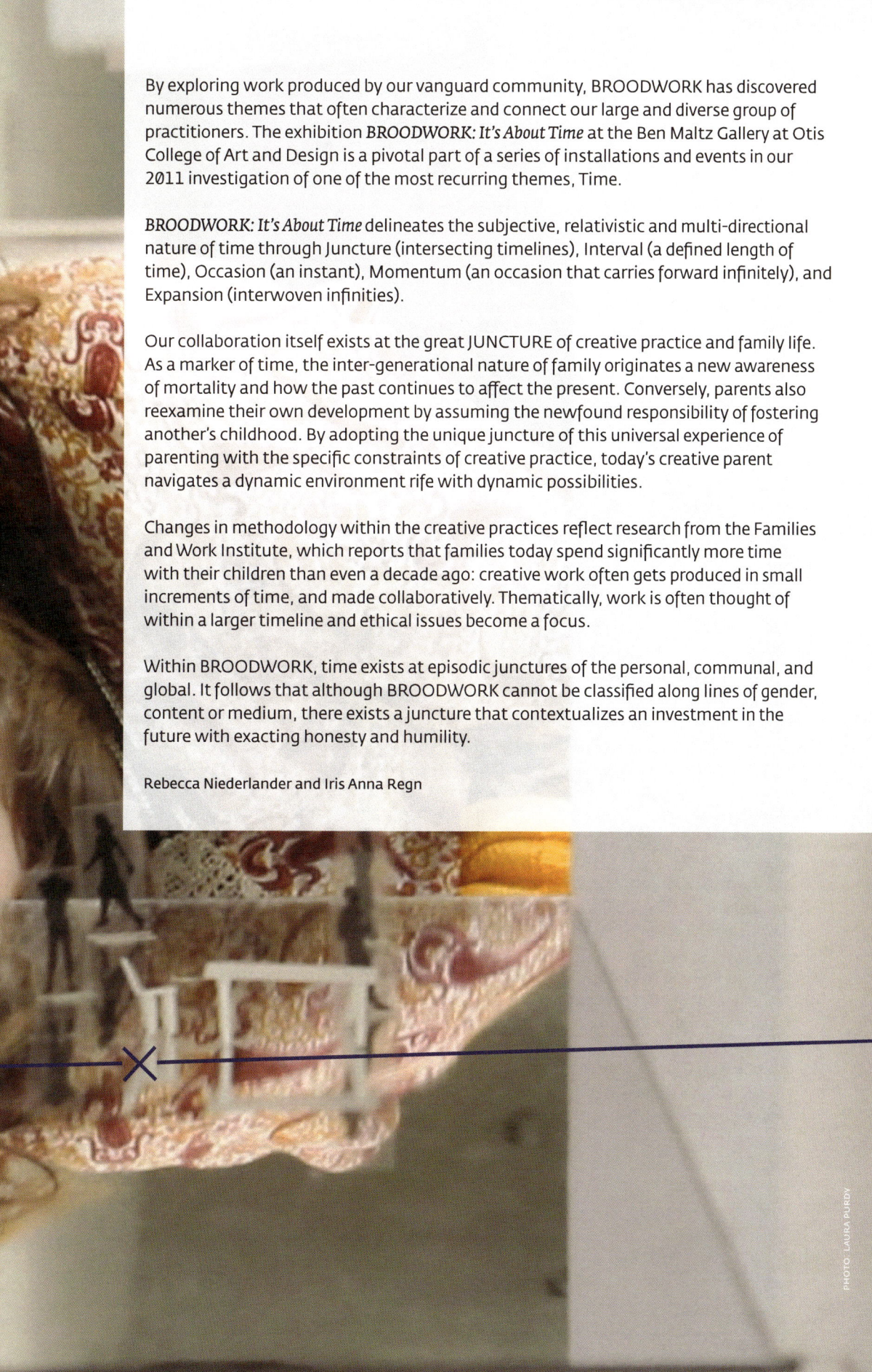

By exploring work produced by our vanguard community, BROODWORK has discovered numerous themes that often characterize and connect our large and diverse group of practitioners. The exhibition BROODWORK: It's About Time at the Ben Maltz Gallery at Otis College of Art and Design is a pivotal part of a series of installations and events in our 2011 investigation of one of the most recurring themes, Time.

*BROODWORK: It's About Time* delineates the subjective, relativistic and multi-directional nature of time through Juncture (intersecting timelines), Interval (a defined length of time), Occasion (an instant), Momentum (an occasion that carries forward infinitely), and Expansion (interwoven infinities).

Our collaboration itself exists at the great JUNCTURE of creative practice and family life. As a marker of time, the inter-generational nature of family originates a new awareness of mortality and how the past continues to affect the present. Conversely, parents also reexamine their own development by assuming the newfound responsibility of fostering another's childhood. By adopting the unique juncture of this universal experience of parenting with the specific constraints of creative practice, today's creative parent navigates a dynamic environment rife with dynamic possibilities.

Changes in methodology within the creative practices reflect research from the Families and Work Institute, which reports that families today spend significantly more time with their children than even a decade ago: creative work often gets produced in small increments of time, and made collaboratively. Thematically, work is often thought of within a larger timeline and ethical issues become a focus.

Within BROODWORK, time exists at episodic junctures of the personal, communal, and global. It follows that although BROODWORK cannot be classified along lines of gender, content or medium, there exists a juncture that contextualizes an investment in the future with exacting honesty and humility.

Rebecca Niederlander and Iris Anna Regn

# CMMNGRND

## 2011
CONCEPTUAL MODEL, MIXED MEDIA

We started our office somewhere between Amalia and Francis, our two daughters.

In hindsight, it might have been because we did not differentiate very much between work and family, and that we were just ready to explore the possibilities of our own ideas in the real world and to take on the responsibilities.

So we did. We got married, had children, moved out of our mouse heaven east-village studio and opened shop of SO-IL, all at the same time, and all intuitively.

We never got to have the time to think about what kind of parents we wanted to be, nor what kind of architect. We fought the sleepiness through the night feedings by thinking about the window details. We brought the kids along to the numerous site visits on weekends. They were always happy guests at our office dinners and holiday parties, knew the name of every one of our staff members, and proudly invited their friends to the openings of our projects.

There are many ways one can learn to become a parent, or to start an architectural office. Our way took its course rather than being set out by us. The conflicts between the two do not result in compromises, but help us in making wise decisions. We rarely feel the split between the two roles, but one always makes the other more interesting. Sometimes we are impatient waiting for the next step, other times we feel chased by the growth of a child or the office. In time, we learn how to wait for the current and ride it when it comes.

Now our older daughter is 4 years old and the office 3, there came a natural convergent point where we sought to rethink the model of the living spaces, as we increasingly find the over-priced housing market in New York structurally ignores the relational spaces in a residential environment. We wanted to test the viability of an architecture that facilitate a communal oasis in the hyper-urban setting.

Over dinners and tea times, we spoke of this desire and our dream with our "extended families", our diasporic friends who sought for each other in this metropolitan New York. Once planted, how powerful it is, the way in which a seed bursts out of its shell and pierces though the dirt to reach for the light of possibilities! Quickly, the dream grew in an infectious way. Now it has a name, Cmmngrnd. It is a place to work and to live; to support and to depend; to be and to become.

mngrnd

CORINNE VAN DER BORCH AND IWAN BAAN

## CMMNGRND

### 2011
VIDEO

"How to visualize this dream?" Jing and Florian asked me over an 'extended family' christmas dinner…As future *Cmmngrnd* inhabitants, Iwan Baan and myself set out to create a series of video portraits of our *Cmmngrnd* neighbors to be. We chose to shoot in an observational manner-to be as voyeuristic as possible and visualize this dream of '*Cmmngrnd*' by showing its future inhabitants in their current living environment. As a documentary filmmaker, I like to observe people dreaming. Iwan's photography is known primarily for images that narrate the life and interactions that occur within architecture. We are very proud to give you a peek under the tent of a group of people around the world that share a common dream together.

PHOTO: COURTESY SO-IL

# I AM U R ME

**1998**
VIDEO

Michael Jackson's *Black or White* video was the first time I saw that morphing effect. The video concludes with a series of beautiful people of various races and ages morphing from one into another. It was cutting edge entertainment technology applied to a message of global unity. The effect was amazing to me. I desired to apply such a grand statement onto my own tiny life. My art, at that time, was becoming more personal-hyper local, but also more entertaining. I had contrasting desires to address my own life intimately while simultaneously wanting to speak to a wider audience. *I Am U R Me* can be understood from a variety of perspectives: Freudian, Genetic, Cultural, Spiritual. It was also inspired by Charles Ray's *Family Romance* sculpture. The title comes from a Red Hot Chili Peppers song.

TONY TASSET

MICHELLE SEGRE

# UNTITLED 2010

**2010**
METAL, PAPIER-MÂCHÉ, PLASTICINE, CLAY, ROCKS

I think the biggest influence on my work of the last few years has been my kid. His way of looking at art, his completely zany little sculptures that he makes to fill up time-- it's all gotten into my head and totally permeated my approach to art-making. So whatever time in the studio I have lost through childcare, I've made up for it by gaining a creative impulse that is more straightforward and spiritually gratifying than anything I've ever done.

## AB OVO
## AB OVO BINDER

**2006**
BOOK

I was inspired by my children's custody battle for "Ab Ovo" or "From the Egg" and chose to use the children's story as the goal and framework for the piece.

*For Hull's* Ab Ovo *project and book, 19 artists took the Minnesota Multiphasic Personality Inventory. He gave the resulting personality profiles to 19 writers, who each wrote children's story based on the profiles. These stories were given to 19 different artists, who provided illustrations.*

STEVEN HULL

# MOMENTUM

DAVID MULLER

Momentum: the strength or force that allows something to continue or to grow stronger or faster as time passes—an occasion that carries forward infinitely

Moment um: a moment and then the sound of hesitation before the next thought

Mome(n)tu(m): "Môme" is French slang for "kid" and "tu" is French for "you"

We all begin at the starting gate with the "kapow" of birth...and then momentum picks up

                                          keep going keep going keep going
                                          keep doing keep doing keep doing

Momentum is ideal when rhythmic, evolutionary, and path-forging. It is never really smooth with family. Once the impact of the responsibility for others hits, the momentum may slow down; it may pause; it may even feel like it goes in reverse for a bit.

*Nothing created, nothing lost, all is transformed.* —Antoine Lavoisier, 17c chemist

There is zen in stillness but momentum carries you through highs and lows of existence. We work with the best of the past to improve for the future. We learn from parents, from odd jobs and relationships, from accidents and triumphs. We learn from our children.

p_object = mv (p is for momentum; m is mass; v is velocity)

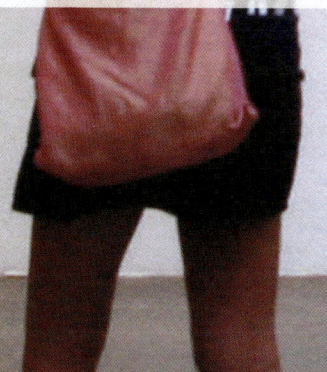

                                                  Create
                                               Spark
                                           Sustain
                                      Maintain
                                 Trigger
                               Find
                          Destroy
                       Lose
                   Generate
               Stimulate
            Develop
         Discover
      Gain
    Gather
Build

Creative thought and productivity come from observational learning, innovative design, and play. We seek discovery and revelation. The elements of surprise are what keep our desires robust.

Keep the momentum of surprise and everything should be fine.

Asuka Hisa

## MULLER FAMILY CAR LISTENING STACK (FROM FRANCES DOWN TO DAVE)

**2011**
ACRYLIC ON PAPER

I try to make some ephemeral things concrete. In this case I'm nailing down a moment when these recordings were together in the one car we own. It covers the Muller family listening spectrum: from the drones of Yoshi Wada and Catherine Christer Hennix (which only Dave likes) through Grizzly Bear and Liz Phair (Dave & Ann like) on to Brenda Fassie and M.I.A. (everyone likes) then The Airborne Toxic Event (only Grace likes) and finally Kanye West and The Little Mermaid OST (only Frances likes). The spectrum runs from Dave at the bottom to Frances at top. This moment is already passed; Spring cleaning has struck. A whole new spectral array starts to assemble itself.

DAVE MULLER

## ABSTRACT CITY BLOG: HAUNTED HOUSEHOLD
## ABSTRACT CITY BLOG: RED EYE

**2010**
INKJET PRINTS

For me the ideal joke consists of the viewer/reader providing 98% of the idea, and the illustration just filling in that last tiny piece of the puzzle, that makes everything come together.

Much of my work certainly wouldn't have happened without the inspiration I am getting from spending time with my kids; but I try to use this light and playful approach merely as a visual Trojan horse to tell a more or less grown-up story. One thing has changed though: since I have kids I can lay on the floor for hours, playing with legos and wooden bricks and pretend that I am actually working.

CHRISTOPH NIEMANN

## PALLET CHAIRS

### 2011
PALLET WOOD
FABRICATED BY VERONICA FRANCO, FRANCISCO J. OSORIO, PORFIRIO J. OSORIO

"Think global, act local" has become a catch phrase for many designers today, and yet viable, effective, and perhaps most importantly, desirable examples of ethical and sustainable design are thin on the ground. Technology is not the enemy here; just as the music and film industries have, albeit out of necessity, experienced a seismic shift to make media more democratic, more interactive, so the design industry needs a radical makeover in its methods of design, production, distribution and consumption to provide a meaningful solution to increasing shortages of materials and rising concerns at the effects of global capitalism. I do not pretend to have the answer to these very big, and very real, problems; nevertheless, with *Pallet Furniture* I have been trying to shift my way of working and thinking of design.

NINA TOLSTRUP

REBECCA CAMPBELL

## FOR FRAGONARD AND MY MOTHER

**2009**
OIL ON CANVAS

This painting was inspired by thoughts of time, heredity, gender, information, the personal and the historic.

The image is of my mother, turning 80 this year, reading in a guest bed she retreats to when dogged by insomnia. This bedroom has looked exactly as it does in this painting since 1971. The mustard stripes and flowers filling the space speak both to the fevers I sweat in this very bed as a child as well as the cultural conflicts my mother weathered the same decade. Hanging above the bed is a print of *The Reader* by Jean-Honore Fragonard. In it a beautiful young girl, painted almost exactly 200 years before this bedroom was decorated, reflects with a book.

While some may consider Fragonard's treatment of the subject flip or transparent what I see is a girl with a book. Complicated with ironic tension created by the relative youth and age of my subjects it is the painting's subtext of collaboration between the women, a passing of intelligence and experience from one generation through the next that lingers. Death will come, in the book and in the bed but it is the circular nature of time that may suggest some comfort

JOYCE CAMPBELL

## TE TANĪWHA

**2010**
GELATIN SILVER FIBER-BASED HAND PRINTS

## TE TANĪWHA

**2010**
DAGUERREOTYPE

I am looking for the Taniwha Hinekōrako
Who lives at Te Reinga and is an ancestor of everyone in the village
She has a home where the two rivers meet
She has another home under a rock called Hinekuia at the base of the falls
Sometimes I think she shows herself
As a serpent
As a woman (look at her basking)
As a waterway
As an eel
I imagine that she hides her huge body in the caves that line the gorge

PHOTO: JOYCE CAMPBELL

WHY do parents feel they don't have enough time with their children?

Our studies find that 75% of parents feel they do not have enough time with their children, up from 66% in 1992. Are these feelings accurate? Our studies—and other studies—show that mothers are spending as much time with their children as they did in the 1970s. And fathers—especially Gen X fathers and Millennial fathers—are spending a lot more time with their children than fathers did in the 1970s.

WHY do children feel less deprived of time with their parents than the parents feel?

Our studies find that 67% of children 8 through 18 years old say they have ENOUGH time with their mothers and 60% say they have ENOUGH time with their fathers. One might think that children, especially older children, don't want to be with their parents as much as parents want to be with them. But our studies show that it is older children—more so than younger children—who want more time with their parents. In fact, among children 13 through 18, 49% say they do NOT have enough time with their mothers and 64% say they do NOT have enough time with their fathers. Children 8 through 12 are also more likely to want more time with their fathers.

These are WHYS the Families and Work Institute seeks to try to answer through research.

MAYBE it's that we tend to think about the amount of time we spend with children as separate from what happens during that time—quality time versus quantity time.

Children don't tend to see the amount of time and what happens during that time as separate. In one study, if given one wish to change the way a parent's work affects their lives, the largest proportion of children did not wish for more time together—as the majority of parents thought they would. Children wished their parents would be less tired and stressed.

As well, our studies find that children would replace the concepts of "quality time" and "quantity time" with "focused time" and "hang-around time."

MAYBE our concepts of time haven't evolved from industrial era concepts to information era concepts.

We feel pressured to keep that factory line moving—to keep running that marathon, especially when so many of us have electronic tethers to work. However, our studies show that as parents, we feel less conflict between work and family lives when we feel we can really focus on our children AND on ourselves.

WHY NOT reinvent our concepts of time so that we are not always chopping time up into packed little intervals? Instead, try to create some time when we are hanging out and some when we are focusing on each other. It's about time we do!

Ellen Galinsky
President, Families and Work Institute

# GLIMPSE

## 2011
VIDEO PROJECTOR, DVD PLAYER, SLIDE PROJECTOR, BLANK SLIDES, CUSTOM ELECTRONICS

About 5 years ago I started making works that incorporated found home movie footage in a liminal way. As the movies were presented in extremely low resolution, none of the details of the images were visible to the viewers giving them a somewhat "universal" home-movie feel. *Glimpse*, which also uses found home movies, presents the films obscured / washed out by the light of a slide projector such that only the beginning of each camera shot is visible. This structure makes *Glimpse* liminal in a different perceptual dimension compared to my other home movie based works. One needs to use short term memory and edge recognition to comprehend the moving imagery of *Glimpse*.

JIM CAMPBELL

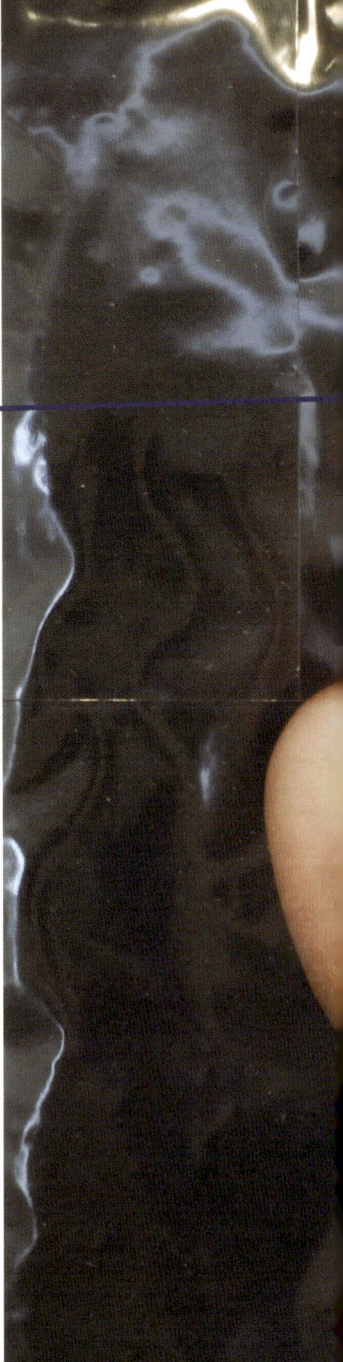

## UNTITLED

### 2010
INKJET PRINTS AND URETHANE FOAM ON PANEL

Balancing on a flat bed scanner, I made a digital image of my fingers, thumbs and toes at a high resolution. This required a certain degree of focus and concentration. The seven minutes required to complete the scan seemed much longer because of the awkward position I had to maintain.

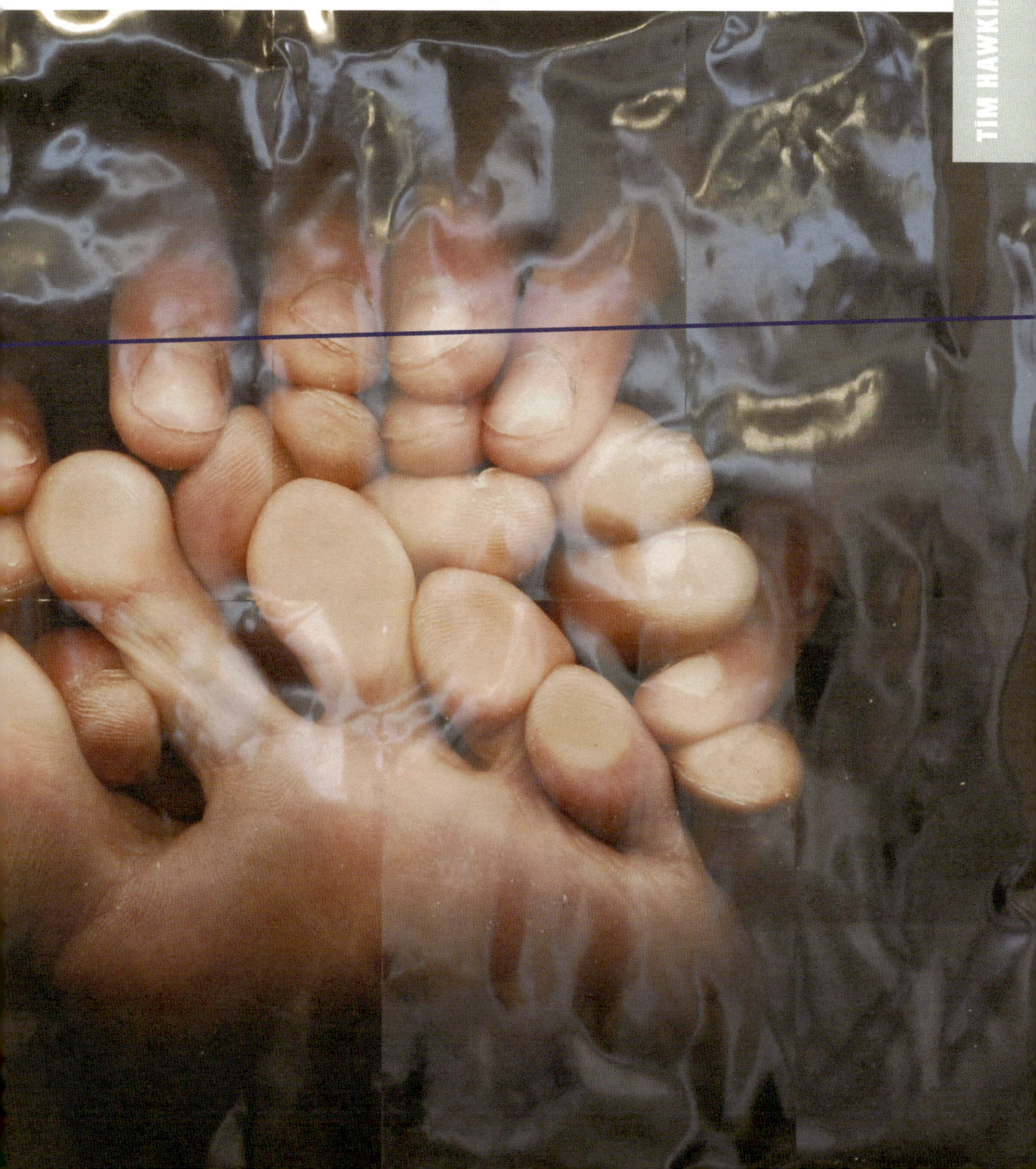

TIM HAWKINSON

## ON RECEIVING THE MESSAGE, AT 3:13 AM ON TUESDAY, SEPTEMBER 21, 2010, THAT JOE SCHRANK HAS CONFIRMED ME AS A FRIEND ON FACEBOOK

**2011**
VIDEO

This work was inspired by the Facebook message alluded to in the title, as well as the advertising for the film *The Social Network*, with which I had been feeling bombarded at the time. The buzz around the movie had inspired a number of ideas in my mind, mostly about the attenuated nature of social networks generally. I tend to feel distant from my networked "friends," and in a sense, it doesn't make much difference whether I know them in "real life," or am merely connected to them through Facebook. It occurred to me, as I contemplated the message from Facebook, that the relationship I was about to begin with Joe Shrank had the potential to be as meaningful as all my other social media relationships. That is, I didn't expect it to be meaningful at all.

As a parent, I am excited when I think of the opportunities that technology will create for my daughter. But I'm also concerned, as a parent and as a global citizen about living in an age where Facebook friendship can represent a connection. On the other hand, I'm aware of philosophies which posit that the information that makes up all of us and all matter is as substantial as the bits and megabytes that swirl around cyberspace. So these two, opposite ideas were battling each other in my head as I wrote. Also, the name "Joe Schrank" sounded funny to me.

1.
A wave of relief washes over me,
As if I had stood at the shore and begged the waters to envelope me,
And the waters granted my wish,
With a whole bunch of water, enveloping me, and I was swept away, by an unusual destiny in the blue sea of August;

And now I am accepted, like the way we all hope to be accepted-by our peers or our audiences or our idols or our deceased descendants,

I am found, like a wretch that once was lost but now is found;

I am redeemed, like a bunch of box tops, plus two dollars and fifty cents postage and handling, mailed in for some talismanic or totemic item tangentially related to Quisp or Kaboom or Lucky Charms;

I am validated, like a driver with a temporary permit to park in a space where she otherwise would not be permitted to park, but now temporarily can, because she has purchased goods or services from a business entity that has been granted the mystical power of parking validation;

I exist, like the sound of a tree that falls in the forest when someone, someone named Joe, is there in the forest to hear it.

The John Hall, who before this moment, was a single Facebook member with a mere 453 Facebook friends, is now not only a Facebook member with 454 friends, but also a part of a 1544 member community-the community of Facebook friends of Joe Schrank.

2.
Perhaps Facebook puts it best when it simply states, "Joe Schrank confirmed you (meaning me) as a friend on Facebook" followed by a dot dot dot

Those ellipses-are they a suggestion of wonderful times ahead? Will my Facebook friendship with Joe Schrank, now in its infancy, grow into a mature, mutually beneficial relationship? Perhaps.

As far as I know, Joe has no band to promote. Perhaps this Facebook Freindship won't be a one-sided, parasitic affair. I dont mean "affair" in the sexual sense. Maybe I don't mean affair at all. Maybe I don't know what I mean.

3.
Perhaps this is a good time to mention that I don't know Joe Schrank, and he does not know me. At all. We have never met in this, the allegedly non-virtual world—
Although maybe the lives we think we live are merely more virtual experience, perhaps of an other, possibly higher, order.

4.
Point being though,
I have never laid eyes on Joe Schrank;
Never heard his voice or smelled his scent.
Never pressed the flesh
Never shot the breeze
We've never gone fishing together,
Never discussed anything,
Never meditated
Never prayed together.
We've never sucked each other's cocks or
Fucked each other's wives.

I don't even know if Joe is gay or straight, married, single, divorced, childless or childed.
I don't know jack shit about Joe.
I don't know jack shit about Joe.
I don't know jack shit about Joe.

5.
I only requested Joe
On someone else's say so.
Someone who I actually know.
Someone who told me I ought to know Joe.
So there you go.
And here we are.
I waited for a while
And suddenly
Joe Shrank graciously accepted me.
But who is he?
And what should I do now?
Maybe I'll rape his friend list and see if there's anyone there that might like me.

Maybe I'll send him a message
Maybe I'll give him a poke.
Maybe I'll send him some political links.
Maybe I'll tell him a joke

But most likely
He'll sit there
Like most of my other 453 friends
And we won't hear from each other
Or even think about each other
Until Facebook tells us our birthdays are coming up,
Unless of course, somehow, some way, somebody lets Joe Shrank know
About this long long Joe Schrank song.

Joe Schrank
Joe Schrank
Joe, Joe, Joe...

# OCCASION

MICHAEL WORTHINGTON

Do we have time for beauty? In *De Re Aedificatoria*, Leon Battista Alberti defined beauty as "that reasoned harmony of all the parts within a body, so that nothing may be added, taken away, or altered, but for the worse." The reasoned harmony that Alberti posits as a necessary condition for beauty collapses in the face of unreasonable demands on our time. If we do everything that Alberti tells us it will make it worse. We add, we alter, we take away, and we're left with a most irrational, temperamental result with little resemblance to the perfect whole. Under the impetus of these stresses, what should be familiar and homey is made grotesque and unrecognizable.

The *Vitruvian Man* by Leonardo da Vinci furnishes the classic diagram of proportional beauty, the masculine body inscribed in a circle and a square, but he's a lonely paradigm of perfection. No mate or family or friend could be added to this reasoned harmony. He remains locked in his immobile stance, reaching for an unattainable state of balance. By contrast, we live in a realm that perhaps lacks Cartesian order, but is full of people and of occasions for creating un-beautiful work. In this world, the ideal of beauty is fragmented, dissected, recombined, distorted, replicated, warped, transported. You might say the occasional replaces the beautiful.

Pat Morton

## LYRIC POSTER: CATERPILLAR GIRL
## LYRIC POSTER: KOOKS
## LYRIC POSTER: PUT THE BOOK BACK ON THE SHELF

**2011**
INKJET ON PAPER

A different house, seven years ago now. My daughter cries, I hold her close to my shoulder. It's nighttime, I'm lightheaded from tiredness. I dance her in my arms around the large glass table in the center of the room. Round and round and round, simultaneously rocking side to side, bouncing, and moving forward… round and round. I can't sing, but I sing for her. Mumbling, repetitive, humming rhymes, round and round… hoping to instill my music in her head early on, hoping she will love the things I love. Each loop of the song quieter than the last. Lyrics dissolve into repetitive do-be-do's, that slip into humming, then humming slips into silence, and silence into sleep.

MICHAEL WORTHINGTON

## DOG SHELF

**2009**
ROTOMOLDED PLASTIC CHILDREN'S TOYS

## TOY FURNITURE

**2009**
DOCUMENTARY FILM

When my son Jasper and daughter Sophia were small children, my family consumed and discarded numerous large scale rotomolded plastic toys. Recycling these toys into building elements, furniture and objects of use was the inspiration. They outgrew the toys but now we get to preserve them as functional mementos.

GREG LYNN

# ORION'S SECOND MONTHS

## 2009
DRAWINGS ON PAPER

Drawings about the present quickly become works about the past.

DANICA PHELPS

# EXPANSION

**HEALTH AND BEAUTY**

So here we are.

I'm staring at my computer, you're staring at some text on a page. But through a collapse in the time/space continuum, here we are together. While writing this in my broken armchair, I'm handling too many things at once: a chilly paper cup of coffee, the collected works of Antonin Artaud (edited by Susan Sontag), deadlines and remiss correspondences, and the provocative antics of a wise-cracking girl-child (five and three-quarters by last reckoning), all the while listening to Becky Stark of Lavender Diamond croon as if just for me "Dream the kind of a life that you will find. The kind of love that lasts forever."

I'm glad you took the time to be here, what with the demands of life on your end too. Don't worry, this won't be another complaint about the pace of modern life, how all the hours get tapped away in bits of work and bits of chores, and a moment for this and that, and that moment between this and that where you just need to rest and check to see if you've any messages. Dictated by digital fingers of a creeping clock, full of fast paced triviality, this life (and our complaints of it) can so easily feel so full of nothing but its own rapid pacing.

But time is really whatever we want it to be.

This is hopefully more about the strange space of time, how it folds and contracts into cozy nooks for hurried moments of affection, how it spreads and expands to encompass hundreds of generations of human struggle into a graceful instant. How time, running away in all directions, can be caught and savored, and rather than battled against, how easily the running of time can be simply enjoyed. Hopefully, this is more about how unscheduled whimsicality can puncture the assembly line of schedules.

Just now, and you wouldn't know it, I took a break for a dance party with the girl-child, we waltzed across the office/bedroom/ballroom, cheek-to-cheek, her hair smelling like strawberries, feet dangling at my waist. The words you're now reading are much lighter than the words you read before, much more expansive than all the sentences that came before it. The lightness of that impromptu dance, however fleeting, will endure, a good and worthy moment to be alive. It made writing this so much easier, perhaps even made writing this worthwhile. It lent conviction, however lissome, to what might have otherwise been mere words, heavy and heaving with their own self-importance. A stolen frolic of quiet domestic bliss, paternal bewonderment, simple humanity. A moment of shared time.

Now back to life for both of us. You'll close the book, check your phone, worry about traffic, and I'll press a button and send this off. I apologize for how one-sided our relationship has been, but as far as can tell, it seems to have gone well.

I'm glad we could spend this time together.

Andrew Berardini

## A HISTORY OF PLAY: FROEBEL EAMES STUDIO

### 2011
MIXED MEDIA INSTALLATION

The work in this exhibition grew directly out of my relationship with my family. In the Fall of 2008, my wife borrowed the book *An Eames Primer* by Eames Demetrios. I read the book over the period of the following week during journeys on the bus to and from my studio. I learned that Charles Eames (and Frank Lloyd Wright, Le Corbusier, Mondrian and others) was educated in early childhood using the method developed by Frederich Froebel, who also invented Kindergarten. Our son Emil is five years old and Mikkel is three. They provide a constant flow of joy and inspiration, and continually prove that play is at the root of all creativity. Becoming a parent opened my eyes up to not only my parents' influence on us as children (they are both artists and three of my five siblings are also artists, one is a curator) but also how life and art and striking a balance is a continual process and should be approached as such. Therefore I have learned to slow down and enjoy life much more and to let it influence my work as an artist and an educator in a much more fluid and intuitive way.

EAMON O'KANE

**BALLET FOR MARTHA: MAKING APPALACHIAN SPRING** 2010
**ACTION JACKSON** 2008
**CHRISTO AND JEANNE-CLAUDE: THROUGH THE GATES AND BEYOND** 2008
**RUNAWAY GIRL: THE ARTIST LOUISE BOURGEOIS** 2003
**VINCENT VAN GOGH: PORTRAIT OF AN ARTIST** 2001
**FRANK O. GEHRY: OUTSIDE IN** 2000
**CHUCK CLOSE: UP CLOSE** 1998
**THE AMERICAN EYE: ELEVEN ARTISTS OF THE TWENTIETH CENTURY** 1995
**THE SCULPTOR'S EYE: LOOKING AT AMERICAN ART** 1993
**THE PAINTER'S EYE: LEARNING TO LOOK AT CONTEMPORARY AMERICAN ART** 1991

JAN GREENBERG AND SANDRA JORDAN

Our books have to do with passion for the arts, collaboration, and the creative process.

We met in 1978 when Jan submitted the manuscript for her first children's novel, *A Season In Between*, to Farrar, Straus & Giroux where Sandra was then Editor-in-Chief of Children's Books. More than ten years of friendship later we hatched the idea for *The Painter's Eye* and decided to focus on postwar American art. Not only was this topic a gap in the bookshelf (every nonfiction writer's dream), but also we could talk to living artists about subjects we thought would interest young readers.

Our tenth book, *Ballet for Martha: Making Appalachian Spring*, began with a trip to the awesome Isamu Noguchi Garden Museum in Long Island City to see an exhibit of Noguchi's stage sets. The famed sculptor did 37 set designs for dance and theater. More than twenty of them were for Martha Graham. Our conversations kept leading us back to his set for *Appalachian Spring* and the collaboration between Noguchi, Martha Graham (dance), and Aaron Copeland (music). The piles of biographies on our desks grew higher. And, of course, we interviewed dancers, musicians, and conductors for insights into this American classic. Since we are collaborators, we were curious about how Martha worked with her troupe, as well as with Aaron, the composer, and with Isamu, the sculptor. And the love story of the young farmer and his bride, who celebrate their wedding day and the completion of their new home in Appalachian Spring, is very compelling. The dance captures the energy of the pioneer spirit, of America in its early days.

We live in different places and have very different lives, but we love getting together for a new project. We've continued to ask snoopy questions throughout the years we've worked together.

# IT'S ALL ONE THING

## 2011
100 NOTEBOOKS

Subject: Venerable Lama Chodak Gyatso Nubpa, parinirvana
Date: Wed, 14 Oct 2009 20:51:53 -0700

hi son
This is the lama I have been working with for the last 7 years on various projects in Tehachapi.

He was very sick the last 6 months with a flare up of recurring hepatitis he got in india many years ago. Even when he was ill, he still served. The last time I saw him was 4 months ago in Tehachapi where the mandala will be built one day.

He was suffering but doing all he could to camouflage it. What a gift it has been to be able to spend time with someone who embodies such compassion and wisdom and totally a 'cool' guy. We had wonderful conversations and walks around the canyon site talking of so many things. One time as our conversation focused on the design of buildings on the site, he asked me, "what should they look like," trying to help him understand the limits of 'style' I responded, "they should be invisible." He stopped in his tracks and turned to me and asked me to explain how this was possible, I turned and pointed to a huge extra ordinary cedar tree that we had just walked by without noticing it and said that this tree was an example of invisibility- it was hiding in plain sight. Again he asked me to elaborate. I continued that this tree, in its full character had become what it was because of its context which created the conditions for this tree to manifest as it did. It was inevitable.

Inevitability and invisibility are the same. He smiled in a way that made it evident that he already knew this. I realized that what I had just said, having spoken extemporaneously, was inevitable as well.

The context of being there at that moment in that natural environment walking and talking with him created the conditions for these thoughts which I had the opportunity to express another mini-epiphany.

Being around some people, you can not help but learn. True learning is an act of discovery of something that was always present.

I am sad at the moment but reflective.

It helps being so close to nature, here in Kyoto. The campus is in the hills on the edge of a forest. I went for a walk among the huge cedars this morning, and thought of the lama.

I love you very much and miss you.

Mr

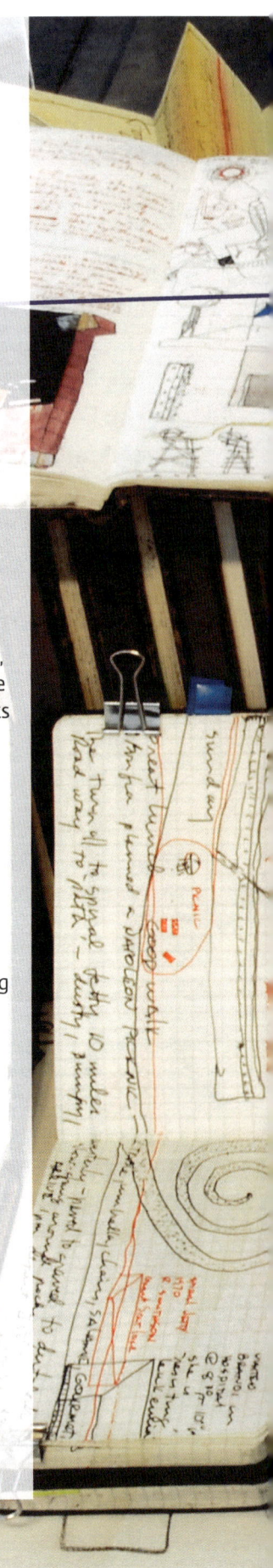

MICHAEL ROTONDI

**FINISHING SCHOOL**
JAMES ROJSIRIVAT
BRIAN BOYER
JOEL HEFLIN
JASON PLAPP
ED GIARDINA

### M.O.L.D.

#### 2009
MIXED MEDIA

*M.O.L.D.* is a hot zone-themed performance, installation and workshop that investigates food in crisis. Specifically, the science, politics, and culture of food decomposition. The audience is invited to participate in various experiments, build their own amateur bioindicators, and engage in a critical conversation about the quality and safety of the food we all consume. The *M.O.L.D.* project grew from a series of casual conversations between collective members about what they feed their young children and why.

### THE SAGE TABLE

#### 2011
MIXED MEDIA

*The Sage Table* is part of a movable feast - a distribution of food and information. This communal table is a mobile planting surface, site for meals, museum, library, granary and a place for gathering. The table is charged by the archetype of the family dinner table - a site of growth, a site of interaction, and a site of learning through generational exchange. A hand painted map hanging above the table charts the City of Los Angeles as a host for the table through time, connecting its past, present, and future sites. As the table moves around the city, it will continue to grow seasonal edibles for harvesting; as the availability of produce is one of the most apparent way of understanding the passing of seasonal time in Los Angeles. Participants in this first installation of *The Sage Table* include Katie Bachler, Allison Danielle Behrstock, Janica Ley, Shatto Light, Edie Kahula Pereira, and Michael Pinto.

**PROJECT FOOD LA**

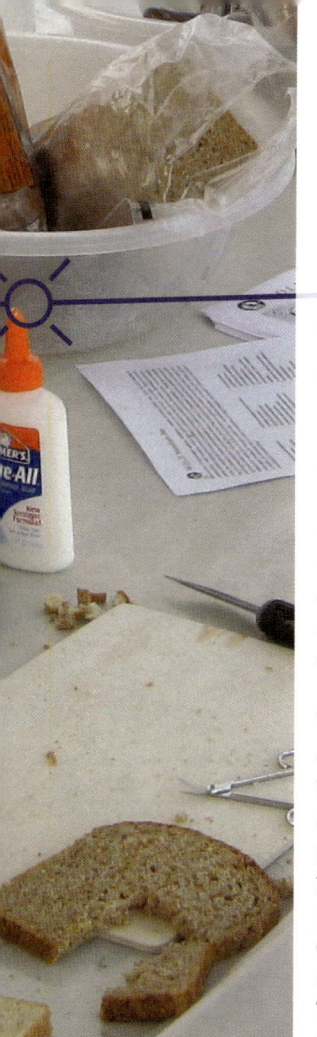

## FOUR PIECES FOR COURTYARD AND ELEVATOR

### 2011
MIXED MEDIA

Health and Beauty is an ensemble exploring the realm between chance and strategy, combining analog, digital and acoustic sources into dense, elastic sound constructions. Each performance is site and context specific.

We began simply, as many bands do, with informal after-hours jam sessions. Two became three, then four, as we gradually added more members, until at present the band hovers between six and seven players. The ensemble has coalesced much the way families do, growing over time, accommodating each new individual and perspective along the way. At a certain point we became actual family, when Paul's brother Eriks joined the group. *BROODWORK: It's About Time* also gave us the opportunity to include a guest musician, Lance's daughter Amanda. Her participation compelled us to investigate new forms, bringing a new layer of discourse to our sonic dialog, much the way every generation asks the previous generation to open up to new possibilities.

HEALTH AND BEAUTY

TIM DURFEE
MARK GEE
LANCE GLOVER
CLANCY PEARSON
ERIKS VITOLINS
PAUL VITOLINS

PHOTO: MEG LINTON

**BROODWORK: MARKING TIME**

ABIRA ALI
ANN FAISON
ILAAN EGELAND MAZZINI
ALLA KAZOVSKY

A *Cause for Creativity* event at Santa Monica Museum of Art in conjunction with *BROODWORK: It's About Time*.

BROODWORK has orchestrated the following set of activities to encourage participants into understanding family as a mechanism for marking time by navigating the spaces of the individual, the family, and the larger extended family that is the City.

### MAKING TIME

Ann Faison leads the adults in breathing exercises to move them from the defined space of the individual to the open-ended experience of drawing. The easiest, most direct way to shift our experience (of time, of ourselves, of our city) is to change our perspective. One way is to shift our breathing. Through breathing meditation, or pranayama yoga, we concentrate our minds on the breath and clear the mind. We then get the gift of deep connection to the self. When that happens, time stops. We realize the connectedness of all things. We have made time.

Ilaan Egeland Mazzini and Carol McDowell of Family Dance Jam lead movement games and dance explorations using an array of found and repurposed materials to play; we freeze time, expand space, shift direction and change shape. We listen to our impulses through simple warm-ups activities readying ourselves to build community dances together. To finish we devise prop filled environments for open-ended fun.

### MAPPING TIME

Architect Alla Kazovsky conducts a creativity workshop, which utilizes strategies of mind mapping with collage to build current and ideal scenarios. "The love of anything is the fruit of our knowledge of it, and it grows as our knowledge deepens," wrote Leonardo da Vinci. This workshop is based on the premise that the brain is equipped to match the image with performance. Through collage, participants learn a technique of visualizing aspirations and their impact. By investigating, uncovering, and noting the origin of interdependent relationships (integrated systems) that make up individual and collective reality, we create a mind map for achieving what we want.

Abira Ali, Katherine Coyle, Gordon Henderson, and Lydia Vilppu of Wisdom Arts Laboratory lead children in the evolution of a tiny town that encourages whimsical untraditional interpretations of building surface, and unusual figures to inhabit the spaces that we create.

### MARKING TIME

Participants are given the Four Rules for Route-Making of Dan Koeppel's Big Parade and encouraged to create communal itineraries of the great, extended family that is their city.

PHOTO: ASUKA HISA

# THANK YOU

Thank YOU for making this exhibition possible and supporting the integration of creative practice and family life!

SPONSORS
Culture Ireland
Pasadena Art Alliance

Thank you to our families who encourage and support us.
A very special thank you to Tim and Milla and Mike and Celeste.

PHOTO: IRIS ANNA REGN

Ameringer McEnery Yohe, Dan Boer, Blum and Poe, Ellen Galinsky, Brennan & Griffin, Daniel Weinberg Gallery, Durfee Regn, Finishing School, FORM, Handbuilt Studio, Health and Beauty, Herman Miller, Inc, Hosfelt Gallery, Kavi Gupta CHICAGO I BERLIN, LA Louver, Little Flower Candy Company, Heather McGinn, Marg Morgan, Francisco Osorio, Veronica Franco, Porfirio J. Osorio, OTIS Information Systems, Dan Rossiter, Santa Monica Museum of Art, SO-IL, Anne Swett, Eddie Urfano, Bob Walters, Joshua Weir

OTIS
Otis College of Art and Design prepares diverse students of art and design to enrich our world through their creativity, their skill, and their vision.

Board of Trustees
Thomas R. Miller (Chair), Susan Crank (Vice Chair), Rodney Freeman (Vice Chair), Bob McKnight (Vice Chair), Gail Buchalter, Stephanie Cota, Bettye Dixon, Bronya Pereira Galef (Chair Emerita), Elaine Goldsmith (Chair Emerita), Samuel Hoi (ex officio), Steve Jarchow, Lawrence Lyttle, Jennifer Bellah Maguire, Winifred White Neisser, F Ronald Rader (ex officio), Jim Rygiel ('81), Michael S. Smith, Christopher Wicks, Wendy Wintrob, Roger Wyett

Board of Governors
F Ronald Rader (Chair), Pat Kandel (Immediate Past Chair), Steven Abram, Nelson Algaze, Judy Bernstein (ex officio), Helen Bolsky, Sibyl Buchanan, Eric Egaas, Steven Ehrlich, Christine Elia, James Evans, Frederick Fisher, Ann R. Gooding ('87, MFA), Barbara Horwitz, Elaine Tajima Johnston, Shannon Loughrey, Laura Maslon, Shelley E. Reid, Gregory Rovenger, Jean Smith, Adrianne Zarnegin

Ben Maltz Gallery
Meg Linton (Director of Galleries and Exhibitions), Jinger Heffner (Exhibition Coordinator and Gallery Registrar), Kathy MacPherson (Gallery Manager and Outreach Coordinator), Paige Tighe (Curatorial Fellow), Joanne Mitchell (Curatorial Intern), Philip Weil (Preparator), Kurt Chang (Gallery Intern), Gabrielle Levine (Gallery Intern), Julia Marasa (Gallery Intern)

PHOTO: LAURA PURDY

# OTIS Otis College of Art and Design

ISBN 0-930209-24-9
©2011 Ben Maltz Gallery, Otis College of Art and Design
9045 Lincoln Boulevard, Los Angeles, CA 90045
www.otis.edu/benmaltzgallery
galleryinfo@otis.edu
Tel. +1 310 665 6905

This catalogue is published in conjunction with the exhibition BROODWORK: *It's About Time*, April 30-June 11, 2011 organized by the Ben Maltz Gallery at Otis College of Art and Design and funded, in part, by Culture Ireland and the Pasadena Art Alliance.

All rights reserved. No part of this book may be reproduced in any form by any electronic or mechanical means (including photography, recording, or information storage and retrieval) without permission in writing from the publisher.

Designer: Yuju Yeo, Handbuilt Studio
Editors: Meg Linton, Rebecca Niederlander, Iris Anna Regn
Printer: Createspace
Photo Credits: Chris Warner unless noted otherwise
Cover Image: Front, Handbuilt Studio; Back, Greg Lynn
Thank you page: Steven Hull; Eamon O'Kane